STAND
— on the —
WORD
Study Guide

EPHESIANS

KEEP
STANDING!

A 7-Day Journey through the Word
with Tony Perkins

FIDELIS PUBLISHING ®

ISBN: 9781956454659

Ephesians: Keep Standing!
A Stand on the Word Study Guide

© 2023 Tony Perkins

Content contributor: Dr. Kenyn Cureton
Cover design: Diana Lawrence
Interior layout design/typesetting: Lisa Parnell
Copyeditor: Lisa Parnell

Order at www.faithfultext.com for a significant discount. Email info@fidelis publishing.com to inquire about bulk purchase discounts.

Fidelis Publishing, LLC Winchester, VA • Nashville, TN

www.fidelispublishing.com

Unless noted otherwise, Scripture quotations are taken from the New King James Version®. Copyright © 1982 by Thomas Nelson. Used by permission. All rights reserved. (Words in italics are additions in the original text.)

Manufactured in the United States of America

10 9 8 7 6 5 4 3 2 1

Contents

— DAY 1 —
Ephesians: An Introduction

Welcome to the Stand on the Word study guide on Ephesians! This letter is certainly one of the most important writings of the apostle Paul, who is universally accepted by credible New Testament scholars as the author. The letter to the churches in Ephesus is one of my favorite sections of Scripture. In fact, this letter contains my life verse: "Therefore take up the whole armor of God, that you may be able to withstand in the evil day, and having done all, to stand" (6:13). Before we dive into our study of the text, let's consider the background and a brief overview of Ephesians.

Background

Ephesus was the capital of Asia Minor, so it was a political center—in fact Rome had made it a free city. It also was a religious center. The temple of the goddess Diana, or Artemis, was located there and is one of the seven wonders of the ancient world. Underneath the statue was one of the largest bank vaults of the day. So the city was a financial hub, and all kinds of trade flowed in and out, by the river and roads that brought goods in from the interior to the busy harbor that shipped them out. Business was booming. GDP was strong. Consequently, Ephesus was not only a political and religious center; it was also a commercial center. Multiplied thousands of local and foreign people crowded its streets.

Ephesus also became a strategic place in the spread of the gospel, and God led Paul to start a church there. All told, Paul stayed a total of nearly three years according to Acts 19–20. In the early years, Priscilla and Aquila labored there. The eloquent Bible teacher Apollos was converted and ministered in Ephesus. Paul's apprentice in the ministry, Timothy, also spent time there. Apparently, John the apostle served as pastor of the church until he was taken away during the persecution and exiled on Patmos. And the first letter from the risen Lord to the seven churches in Revelation is addressed to Ephesus. So it was a strategic city, and the church was a significant work. It is not surprising Paul felt compelled by the Spirit of God to write to the believers in Ephesus while he was in prison in Rome sometime around 60–62 AD.

Overview

Unlike Paul's letters to the Thessalonians, Galatians, Corinthians, and Philippians, the letter to the Ephesian believers is on the other end of the spectrum when it comes to Paul sharing personal information or addressing specific problems. This is a big picture letter. Paul divided it into two clear segments: (1) the doctrinal section on the foundation of the church in chapters 1–3 and (2) the practical section on the function of the church in chapters 4–6.

In the first part, Paul contended that through faith in Christ we are placed in corporate solidarity with Christ. In fact, he repeatedly referred to believers as being "in Christ." As a result, the believer's position as having been chosen, elected, predestined, etc., by God can only be understood in light of our union with Jesus, who was chosen by God and predestined before the foundation of the world to die as a sacrificial substitute, be raised in triumph, and is now at the right hand of God. And because of this union, Paul said believers are raised from spiritual death with Christ by the mercy of God and even now are seated in the heavenlies in Christ (2:4–6). This positional truth is all a result of God's grace by means of our faith (2:8–9).

Paul's focus was not only on the individual in Christ but also on the body of believers, the church, and its foundation. Ephesians, perhaps more than any other New Testament book, presents the purpose and plan of God for this body, the church. The first three chapters describe God's purpose from eternity past to create a holy community, chosen in Christ, adopted as sons and daughters of God—Jews and Gentiles alike. And now this mystery of the ages has been revealed in how the gospel brings this diverse group into a unified church.

Ephesians 4:1 provides the hinge of the letter: "I, therefore, the prisoner of the Lord, beseech you to walk worthy of the calling with which you were called." After laying out profound theological truths in the first half of the book, in chapters 4–6, Paul challenged the Ephesians and all believers to apply the positional truths of the first three chapters to practical living. Consequently, in these three chapters, Paul moved from the foundation of the church to the function of the church. Specifically, he addressed how we are to live out these lofty truths in our relationships within the church, in the home, at work, and in the world. In the final chapter, Paul addressed the spiritual dimension of the battle in which we are engaged and encouraged believers to be strong in the Lord and in the power of His might, prayerfully put on God's armor. He then concluded with the call to stand and keep on standing. In fact, this is the theme of the letter and of my life: Keep Standing!

How to Get the Most from the Study Guide

While the study guide offers spiritual insights and applications, the real impact comes from the words of Scripture, which is the Word of God. Please read the selected text for the day in your own Bible. God's Word is living and active (Heb. 4:12). The Spirit of God uses His Word to change your life. Nothing else can do that. So before reading the daily commentary, read God's Word! In fact, here are five habits to cultivate as you approach God's Word each day.

1. *Read it through:* Don't skip around. Read the entire selection of Scripture. If you are pressed for time, please read the Bible before you read the study guide notes. So read it through.

2. *Think it over:* Meditate on it. Let it marinate in your mind. If you can, take notes. A notes page is at the end of each day. Think it over.

3. *Pray it in:* Personalize the Scripture. Turn the verse that speaks to you into a prayer, then pray it into your life. Ask God what you need to do in response. This leads to the next habit.

4. *Live it out:* Consider ways to apply what God is revealing to you, ways you can obey Him. Put His word into practice. Make it a part of who you are, how you think, how you speak, and behave toward God and other people. In other words, take God's Word and live it out.

5. *Pass it on.* Don't keep it to yourself. People are in your life who need the same truth God has spoken to you in His Word. Share it. Pass it on.

About Stand on the Word

Stand on the Word is a ministry of Family Research Council, whose mission is to advance God's kingdom by championing faith, family, and freedom in public policy and the culture from a biblical worldview. The purpose of Stand on the Word is to lay the foundation for a biblical worldview through daily reading and application of God's Word. For the daily journey, we have created a chronologically prioritized reading plan through the entire Bible that can be accessed at frc.org/Bible or simply by texting the word *Bible* to 67742.

— DAY 2 —
Today's Reading: Ephesians 1

Verse of the Day

> And He put all things under His feet, and gave Him to be
> head over all things to the church, which is His body, the
> fullness of Him who fills all in all.
>
> *Ephesians 1:22–23*

Please read the entire Scripture selection in your own Bible and highlight
or underline verses that stand out to you before you read the observations
and engage the questions below.

This first chapter of Ephesians covers the foundation of the church and the revelation of God's plan. Our key verses, which basically summarize the chapter, are Ephesians 1:22–23: "And He put all things under His feet, and gave Him to be head over all things to the church, which is His body, the fullness of Him who fills all in all." Before the foundation of the world, God had a plan to redeem humans from sin for the purposes of God's own glory. This is really the essence of this first chapter, and three points look at the revelation of God's plan.

The first point is the *plan* of God from eternity past. We see this in verse 4a where Paul said, "just as He chose us in Him before the foundation of the world." God's plan was not plan B because of unforeseen complications with humankind. This was the plan of a sovereign, all-knowing, and all-powerful God. This was His plan, and it's what He revealed to Paul. And it's what Paul said is revealed in Christ Jesus.

God's plan is for us to be holy and without blame in a relationship with Him. God wants us to be in a relationship with Him, and that comes through Jesus Christ by His grace. His grace saves us. His love is demonstrated through sending His Son, and in and of itself, this was an act of grace. But that unmerited favor from God offers us forgiveness and redemption that comes from receiving Jesus Christ, His death on the cross, His burial, and His resurrection. So this is the plan of God.

The second point is the *purpose* of God. In the first few chapters, this is the mystery revealed in Christ Jesus that Paul talked about. So what is the purpose of God? It's all for the glory of God. It's *His* glory. This is really not about us. In the church today, we tend to make this about us. It really isn't. Yes, we are the beneficiaries of God glorifying Himself, but it's not, as one of the more popular praise choruses claims, that God did not want heaven without us. This sounds nice. And while we're grateful God sent His Son to die for us, ultimately it's not about us.

While we think we should be at the center of God's world, the reality is that God should be at the center of *our* world. God's plan and purpose certainly includes us, but the focus shouldn't be on us. In the end it is about God. The purpose is to bring God glory. Even when Jesus came to this earth, He said, "Not My will, but Thy will be done." Why? Because it was about the glory of the Father. We see this in Ephesians 1:6a, which says, "to the praise of the glory of His grace." And we see it in verses 12 ("that we who first trusted in Christ should be to the praise of His glory") and 14 ("who is the guarantee of our inheritance until the redemption of the purchased possession, to the praise of His glory"). This is about the glory of God. That's what His purpose is about.

The third and final point is the *provision* of God. Here's where the benefits come. We are the beneficiaries of His love and grace demonstrated by Christ Jesus. The provision of God is there to accomplish His plan and the purpose of bringing glory to Himself. The means, in part, by which He does that is to provide us with every spiritual blessing, and I see seven spiritual blessings in this passage.

1. *God chooses us.* We don't go looking for God. God comes after us and chooses us. I'm not going to get into the subjects of predestination or foreknowledge because they are deep subjects. But here's what we do know without question: God chooses us. He adopts us as sons and daughters.

2. *God redeems us and accepts us through Jesus Christ.* He cleanses us, forgives our sins, and accepts us into fellowship with Him through Jesus Christ.

3. *God revealed the mystery of His will.* Ephesians 1:11 says, "In Him also we have obtained an inheritance, being predestined according to the purpose of Him who works all things according to the counsel of His will." This is revealed in the Old Testament era. They didn't have this understanding of what God was doing. God revealed this in Jesus Christ.

4. *God unifies us with other believers in Jesus Christ.* We're going to see more about this in the next chapter.

5. *God gives us hope and purpose.* We have purpose and meaning in this life through Jesus Christ. And that is part of the spiritual blessing. We're not here aimlessly wandering

around, occupying space, and consuming air. We have a purpose. And what is this purpose? It is to glorify God and to enjoy Him forever.

6. *God gives us an eternal inheritance.* Now I want you to grasp these spiritual blessings we enjoy in this life. Of course, we must deal with persecution and opposition. But this is a down payment; it's just a precursor to the eternal inheritance that is ours in Christ Jesus. How do we know? Because we are joint heirs with Christ. We are the recipients of the work of Jesus Christ, adopted as sons preparing to receive the eternal inheritance. How do we know this is going to happen? That leads us to the last point.

7. *God gives us the Holy Spirit as a seal.* He seals us. I know that's a doctrinal teaching some take issue with. I think we're sealed. I think once we truly accept Jesus Christ as our Lord and Savior, we are sealed by the Holy Spirit into the relationship as a son or as a daughter. He says in verse 14, "who is the guarantee of our inheritance until the redemption of the purchased possession, to the praise of His glory." Now, what does that mean? This is a down payment that is nonrevocable. It is a promise that the rest is coming. And so, the Holy Spirit is really the earnest payment that the inheritance, the fullness of our redemption and glorification, is coming.

So how do we know God can do this? Well, Paul continued, in verses 19–21: "and what is the exceeding greatness of His power toward us who believe, according to the working of His mighty power which He worked in Christ when He raised Him from the dead and seated Him at His right hand in the heavenly places, far above all principality and power and might and dominion, and every name that is named, not only in this age but also in that which is to come." Next time we move to Ephesians 2 and will look at God's revelation and His manifestation of grace, which is part of His plan.

Questions for Reflection and Discussion

1. What are the benefits of those who are "in Christ" according to Paul in chapter 1, and specifically how do we get there (see vv. 12–13)?

2. What did Paul pray that we would come to know (see vv. 15–25)?
   a. Hope to which God called us
   b. Riches of His glorious inheritance in the saints
   c. Immeasurable greatness of His power toward us who believe
   d. All the above

Notes on Today's Bible Reading

— DAY 3 —

Today's Reading: Ephesians 2

Verse of the Day

> For by grace you have been saved through faith, and that
> not of yourselves; it is the gift of God.
>
> *Ephesians 2:8*

Please read the entire Scripture selection in your own Bible and highlight
or underline verses that stand out to you before you read the observations
and engage the questions below.

Ephesians 2 covers the revelation of God's grace. One of the more famous verses in all of Scripture, verse 8 captures the essence of this: "For by grace you have been saved through faith, and that not of yourselves; it is the gift of God." In fact, there are four key points in this pivotal chapter.

First, Paul talked about the default position of humankind, that we are dead in trespasses and sin. Now this condition, left untreated by the antidote of God's grace, administered through faith in Jesus Christ, will result in the second death, which is eternal. That is our default position, but what does this look like?

Paul laid it out in the first part of the chapter. He said we're under the influence of the devil. Ephesians 2:2 describes him as "the prince of the power of the air, the spirit who now works in the sons of disobedience." That is the course of this age. That is the default position. Until the new covenant of grace, that was the general condition of all humankind after the fall. But someone might protest, "Just because you don't serve God doesn't mean you serve the devil. That's pretty harsh, isn't it?" Well Jesus declared in Luke 11:23, "He who is not with Me is against Me, and he who does not gather with Me scatters." You see, we have only two choices: Either we serve God, or we serve the devil. That's what Jesus said.

The second point is the deliverance of God. Look what it says in Ephesians 2:4: "But God, who is rich in mercy, because of His great love with which He loved us." As we saw in chapter 1, God's plan, while we are the beneficiaries of the plan, is not only about us; ultimately it's about God's glory. And in this, it displays His nature and His character. So in saving us by His grace, unmerited favor, He displays His nature and His character because of His great love.

Notice Paul said, "God . . . is rich in mercy." Before we were even aware of our situation, where we were dead in our trespasses and sin, God took the initiative. Our salvation is the result of His initiative, not ours. That's important to note. We talked about this in chapter 1, the sovereignty of God. He chose us. He pursued us.

So we see the default position of humankind, we see the deliverance by God, and third, we see the divine design of God firsthand. Ephesians 2:10 says, "For we are His workmanship, created in Christ Jesus for good works, which God prepared beforehand that we should walk in them." We are the products of God's grace. He wants to show us off as the products of His grace. We are produced through Jesus Christ, and we are prepared for good works. Notice that we're not saved by good works. It doesn't say we are. "For we are His workmanship, created in Christ Jesus for good works"—not by good works, for good works—"which God prepared beforehand that we should walk in them." You see, once we're saved, once we are redeemed by God's grace, we are saved to do good works, to bring glory to God. Works don't save us; rather, works are evidence of our salvation.

Now, the fourth and last point is the destruction or dissolving of division. Look what it says in Ephesians 2:14–17: "For He Himself is our peace, who has made both one, and has broken down the middle wall of separation, having abolished in His flesh the enmity, that is, the law of commandments contained in ordinances, so as to create in Himself one new man from the two, thus making peace, and that He might reconcile them both to God in one body through the cross, thereby putting to death the enmity." What was Paul talking about? The separation between the Jews and the Gentiles and that Jesus Christ, the cross of Christ, brings us together.

Remember in the Old Testament, there was a covenant with the Jewish people, and Gentiles were on the outside. Even here, there's a reference made to the temple where there were the partitions, the middle wall of separation, and the court of the Gentiles. You could not go past that point. There was even a separation of the women and the men. But in Galatians 3:28–29, Paul wrote, "There is neither Jew nor Greek, there is neither slave nor free, there is neither male nor female; for you are all one in Christ Jesus. And if you are Christ's, then you are Abraham's seed, and heirs according to the promise." So Jesus Christ—by His death, burial, and resurrection—brings us all into one family. He brings us into unity, into the promises of God. We see this as Paul wrote we are the temple now. We are being built into the temple. The Holy Spirit lives within us. God meets with individuals in the temples. He's meeting with us in His temple. And there is no division.

Now, let me just say this in the closing thoughts: religion divides. I see it across the world, literally around the world, as I serve on the US Commission on International Religious Freedom. Religion divides, but Jesus unites when we accept God's plan of redemption through Jesus Christ according to His grace. The world is not and cannot be made right by religion, but it can be made right by a relationship with Jesus Christ. And Paul laid out the foundation here.

Questions for Reflection and Discussion

1. How did Paul describe people in their unsaved condition, and how has God responded (see vv. 1–5)?

2. As Paul explained it simply, how is it possible for a person to be saved (see v. 8)?
   a. It is by God's Grace alone.
   b. Through Faith in Christ alone
   c. It is God's Gift alone—not our works.
   d. All the above

Notes on Today's Bible Reading

— DAY 4 —
Today's Reading: Ephesians 3

Verse of the Day

[T]hat the Gentiles should be fellow heirs, of the same body, and partakers of His promise in Christ through the gospel.

Ephesians 3:6

Please read the entire Scripture selection in your own Bible and highlight or underline verses that stand out to you before you read the observations and engage the questions below.

The first three chapters of the book of Ephesians deal with doctrinal issues, the foundation of the church. Today we are discussing the final chapter of this doctrinal section, and the theme is the mystery revealed. Our key verse is Ephesians 3:6, "that the Gentiles should be fellow heirs, of the same body, and partakers of His promise in Christ through the gospel."

I want us to look at the revelation of the *mystery*. The word in the original language refers to a hidden truth. Specifically, Paul talked about things hidden in the counsel of God from before the beginning of time. So what is the mystery? Paul told us right here in Ephesians 3:6: both Jew and Gentile alike would come to faith and be incorporated into the same body through the grace of God that is extended through Jesus Christ.

Now as you know, some Gentiles in the Old Testament feared and followed the God of Israel. Yet there was a difference. In fact, you remember in the temple they were separated. There was a court specifically reserved for the Gentiles. So there was a barrier between Jew and Gentile; however, Jesus removed the barrier.

This was the mystery kept in the counsel of God from before the foundation of the world, that there was going to be this age of grace for the Gentiles to be saved and incorporated into God's family. Paul referred to it as the "times of the Gentiles" in Romans 11:25. When the Jewish people generally rejected Christ because of the hardness of their hearts, the gospel was offered to the Gentiles, and they were generally more receptive to it. Obviously, Paul's argument in Romans 9–11 is that this partial hardening of Israel to the gospel doesn't preclude individual Jews from being saved—after all Paul and the apostles were Jewish—but it prevented the nation from accepting Jesus as Messiah until God's plans for the Gentiles are complete. Indeed, when the time is right, God will restore the Jewish nation, and they will come to faith in Christ, ending "the times of the Gentiles" (see Isa. 17:7; 62:11–12; Rom. 11:26).

Back to Paul's point in Ephesians 3 and this mystery revealed. Through the gospel, God invites both Jews and Gentiles into the same body of believers, into the same fellowship, adopting them both as sons and daughters into His family. As we've talked about before, Paul said in Galatians 3:28, "There is neither Jew nor Greek, there is neither slave nor free, there is neither male nor female; for you are all one in Christ Jesus."

So that is the mystery, but how was it revealed? Let's look at Ephesians 3:5: "Which in other ages was not made known to the sons of men, as it has now been revealed by the Spirit to His holy apostles and prophets." This mystery was revealed by the Holy Spirit, who came upon the church at Pentecost. Ephesians 3:9 says why God revealed this: "and to make all see what is the fellowship of the mystery, which from the beginning of the ages has been hidden in God who created all things through Jesus Christ."

And here's the application: we are to be faithful stewards of this sacred secret, this mystery. Like Paul, we are to make known the offer of God's grace to Jew and Gentile alike. The old dispensation of the law, the old covenant, and the exclusivity of salvation being only for the Jewish people—with the Gentiles being excluded—is obsolete in light of the cross. Now there is a new covenant of grace. Not only Jews but also Gentiles are welcomed into God's kingdom by faith in Jesus Christ.

So this was the revelation of it, but it did more. Look at Ephesians 3:10: "to the intent that now the manifold wisdom of God might be made known by the church to the principalities and powers in the heavenly places, according to the eternal purpose which He accomplished in Christ Jesus our Lord." This multifaceted, multisided, unsearchable wisdom of God was unveiled to both the angels of light and the angels of darkness through the church.

This was a key part of God's purpose. God was "schooling" the spirits through this new spiritual community united in Jesus. In fact, Peter told us the angels were curious about what God was doing (1 Pet. 1:10–12). As they say, "Inquiring minds want to know," and God even lets the angels, good and bad, in on it. He reveals the manifold, literally the multicolored, wisdom of God, speaking of its beauty and perfection, in His body, His church. So this is more of the revealing of the wisdom of God that is beyond searchable, incomprehensible to the human mind, but now revealed to men and angels alike.

Through this grace, through this mystery revealed, we can enter the fellowship of the mystery. But Paul said in Ephesians 6:19–20, "and for me, that utterance may be given to me, that I may open my mouth boldly to make known the mystery of the gospel, for which I am an ambassador in chains." So this unveiling of the hidden things in God, is what allows men, women, and children to understand that God loves them and that we can have a relationship with Him through Jesus Christ. And what does it provide? What is this plan? What is this hidden thing? Look at Ephesians 3:12: "in whom we have boldness and access with confidence through faith in Him." This mystery revealed the ability to boldly access God through Jesus Christ. Why? Because our sins have been atoned for and we have been adopted as the sons and daughters of God into His family.

The second part of this chapter (vv. 14–21) is actually a prayer for the believers in Ephesus. Paul prayed for God to bless them according to the riches of His glory. And then we see in this chapter Paul reminded us that the riches of God's glory are infinite. Sometimes in a land of plenty it is difficult to truly conceive of God's glorious riches.

This reminds me of several years ago when I was working with the State Department as a contractor in their antiterrorism program, and we brought foreign police officers to the country. When the wall came down in eastern Europe with the demise of the Soviet Union, we began training police officers from Poland and Hungary, and then later Czechoslovakia. I especially remember a group of Polish police officers. We brought them to the states and took them to an Albertson's grocery store. I'll never forget the men walking in. They just froze. And some of them began to literally weep. They didn't speak English, so I had to work through an interpreter, but the bottom line was they had never seen so much. They had become accustomed to standing in line, sometimes for hours, just to get whatever meager stock was in the store. Maybe a loaf of bread, maybe some milk. But they had never seen such abundance in all their lives, and they were overwhelmed by it.

You see, sometimes we live not realizing the abundance we have in Christ Jesus. Paul asked God to answer his prayers for the Ephesians according to the riches of His glory, which are infinite. He prayed for their spiritual strength. Through the Spirit, he prayed that Jesus would be completely at home in their hearts, by faith—not just casually walking with Jesus, but they would live in such a way that they would be holy vessels rooted and grounded in love.

Paul wrote a lot about love. We only have one English word for *love*, but the Greek has several words for love. One is *agape* love, which is a benevolent, self-sacrificing love for others. It's not sexual love. And this is a love we should be rooted and grounded in—sacrificing to benefit others. We've read this a lot in Paul's writings; what we do, especially in using our Christian liberty, should be to edify and encourage others, to build them up. We should do all things in love.

Then he prayed for us all to know the expanse of Christ's love for us, which passes knowledge. Paul said that we can't even understand it. It surpasses our knowledge and our ability to comprehend. We can only experience it.

Pastor Adrian Rogers told a story[1] about a group of Napoleon's soldiers who made an impactful discovery in a Spanish dungeon after the Inquisition. They found a skeleton chained to one wall, and on the opposite wall they saw a cross the prisoner had apparently etched into the stone. At the apex of the cross, he had carved the word *height*. At the foot of the cross, was the word *depth*. And on either side of the cross were the words *breadth* and *length*. To this prisoner, the cross gives us the dimensions of God's love that Paul prayed about here in Ephesians 3:17–19. The apostle prayed we would grow in our experience of the incredible love of Christ that was fully, finally, and forever expressed on the cross. Then Paul concluded by praying we should be filled with the fullness of God, a God who loves us so much that He was willing to give up His only Son (see Rom. 8:32).

In these first three chapters, we have studied the doctrinal section of Ephesians. Paul explained the foundation of the church and specifically the revelation of God's plan, the revelation of God's grace, and the revelation of the mystery. In chapter 4, we begin the practical section; we learn about Paul's explanation of how to function as the church in this world.

Questions for Reflection and Discussion

1. What is the mystery of Christ that has been revealed (see vv. 1–6)?

2. What did Paul pray that we would grasp (see vv. 14–19)?
    a. Comprehend the dimensions of being in the faith
    b. Know the love of Christ that surpasses knowledge
    c. Be filled with the fullness of God
    d. All the above

Notes on Today's Bible Reading

Today's Reading: Ephesians 4

Verse of the Day

[A]nd be renewed in the spirit of your mind.

Ephesians 4:23

Please read the entire Scripture selection in your own Bible and highlight or underline verses that stand out to you before you read the observations and engage the questions below.

In chapter 4, we begin the practical section of Ephesians. Here Paul explained the function of the church, which is to walk worthy of the call. Our key verse is Ephesians 4:23, which says, "and be renewed in the spirit of your mind."

As a reminder, Paul wrote this letter along with three other epistles from prison. He was a prisoner in Rome between 62 and 64 AD. The first three chapters of Ephesians deal with the doctrine or the foundation of the church, and the second three chapters deal with the function of the church. I'm not alone in this opinion, but Ephesians is one of if not the most significant letter Paul wrote.

Ephesus was a lost, heathen city. It was the home of the great temple to Diana, the fertility goddess, and prostitutes were in the temple, so the temptation to sexual sin was intense. That was the backdrop to this immoral city. It was a center of Greek culture, but people came there from all over the Roman world. In Asia Minor, Ephesus was where Asia and Europe came together because it was on a major trade route. It was a commercial center, and with it came the temptation for greed and many other sins.

Ephesus was packed with people who needed the gospel of Jesus Christ. It was such a strategic city that Paul spent three years there, which was longer than he spent in any other place. But all of this was the backdrop to the teaching he provided for the Christians there. It was quite a similar culture to what we find ourselves in today, with all its temptations and challenges. So this book is especially relevant to us.

Paul began the second half of this letter with a call to walk with a renewed mind. Once asked on a radio program what was the biggest lesson he had ever learned, Dale Carnegie quickly replied, "By far the most vital lesson I have ever learned is about the importance of what we think. If I knew what you think, I would know what you are. Our thoughts make us what we are."[2] Actually, what he was saying is built on biblical truth. Proverbs 23:7 says, "For as he thinks in his heart, so is he." So it's appropriate Paul began this first discussion on the practical application of the Christian faith with a focus on the mind.

As you might recall from chapter 3, the mystery was the fact God was saving both Gentiles and Jews by grace, through faith into the same body. Paul punctuated this theme of unity in 4:1–16. First, he called for maintaining unity through the virtues of humility, gentleness, long-suffering, and love. Then he declared the basis for that unity: They are one body unified by one Spirit, they have one Lord with one faith and one baptism, and they believe in one God. That is the definition of unity!

Yet Paul made it clear that unity does not mean uniformity. In fact, he went on to explain how the Spirit has given members of the body different grace gifts for various roles within the church with a goal of (1) equipping the saints for the work of ministry, (2) edifying of the body of Christ, (3) unifying everyone in the faith, and (4) maturing them in Christ as the head of a redeemed humanity. It is this redeemed humanity that he explained further in this chapter and on into chapter 5.

Then Paul picked back up the focus on the mind in 4:17. He said don't be futile in our mind. The futile mind is the wasteful, useless, empty-headed depravity. Don't pursue useless things. Why would someone walk in futility? Well, it is the darkened understanding. They're spiritually blind. They're darkened in their understanding. Their understanding is being alienated from the life of God because of the ignorance in them, because of the blindness of their hearts.

The unregenerated person cannot see. How else do you explain politicians, including the president, who are so devoted to abortion they refuse to support a law that would require an abortionist to aid a child born alive after a botched abortion? How else do you explain the transgender craze where you can determine your own gender? In fact, last time I checked, Facebook gives you fifty-eight options as to what your gender might be. Yet Jesus, quoting Genesis, unequivocally declares there's only two (see Gen. 1:27; Matt. 19:4). So who's right? Those comments may get me banned from Facebook. Who knows?

The world's information is doubling every two years. I have more information in my phone than most people had in their entire lives a few decades ago. But even though we have all this information, we lack wisdom and understanding. Proverbs 9:10 says, "The fear of the Lord is the beginning of wisdom, and the knowledge of the Holy One is understanding." Romans 1:22 says, "Professing to be wise, they became fools." So there's this futile mind, and it's caused by a darkened understanding.

But then you must ask the question, How did their understanding become darkened? How did they get into that situation? Well, they were alienated from the life of God. A warning is here of a progression that takes place. Immorality is always on the march. Sin never stands still. And Paul warned believers of the path of the Gentiles, those who deny God; this is the path they take away from Him. See, they were alienated from the life of God because of willful ignorance. They were without excuse.

Romans 2:14–15 goes further, saying, "for when Gentiles, who do not have the law, by nature do the things in the law, these, although not having the law, are a law to themselves, who show the work of the law written in their hearts, their conscience also bearing witness, and between themselves their thoughts accusing or else excusing them." But how do you get to a point of a hardened heart? What does that look like? Well, it's a seared conscience. It's given over to immorality, so this is the futile mind—the mind Paul said to put off, and he said to renew your mind. Get a new mind.

But how is the mind renewed? Well, if you have the mind of the world and are comfortable with the darkened understanding, you really need to ask yourself, *Do I know Jesus?* If you know Jesus, your mind will be enlightened. You've got to hear Jesus. How do you do that? Through faith. And faith comes by hearing the Word of God.

That's why we are doing this personal study. To encourage people. At times people say, "You're a public policy organization in Washington. Why are you encouraging people to read the Bible?" Because that's how people get understanding, when they come to know the truth; when their lives are transformed by the truth, they begin to see reality—what is true and not what the media says. So you've got to learn the truth in Jesus.

A renewed mind is the key to the transformed life. The mind is so important, and to have a renewed mind, we must put off the old mind. Stop living as those who do not know Jesus. Now this requires action on our part. If we don't change the way we think, if we don't put off our old ways, we'll just continue down this path.

Colossians 3:1–2 says, "If then you were raised with Christ, seek those things which are above, where Christ is, sitting at the right hand of God. Set your mind on things above, not on things on the earth." Now how do you do that? Well, in the spirit of your mind, you must choose to put the things of the past behind you. To do so, you must change the way you think and what you think about. This is not the power of positive thinking. It's not turning over a new leaf. It's the transformation by the truth of God's Word. The old maxim goes: Sow a thought, reap an action; sow an action, reap a habit; sow a habit, reap a character; sow a character, reap a destiny.

We've got to choose what we're going to fill our lives with, what we're going to fill our minds with. In Philippians 4:8–9, Paul wrote, "Finally, brethren, whatever things are true, whatever things are noble, whatever things are just, whatever things are pure, whatever things are lovely, whatever things are of good report, if there is any virtue and if there is anything praiseworthy—meditate on these things. The things which you learned and received and heard and saw in me, these do, and the God of peace will be with you."

So like changing out of old clothes and into new ones, Paul challenged every Christian to take off their old humanity and to put on their new humanity, in which the image of God is being restored in true righteousness and holiness (vv. 20–24). Then for the balance of the chapter, he compared the old humanity with God's intention for the new (vv. 25–32). Instead of lying, we are to speak truth. Instead of harboring anger, we should seek reconciliation. Instead of stealing, we should work so we can be generous. Instead of tearing down others, we are to build up others with our words. Instead of seeking revenge, we should forgive even as God in Christ forgave us. The old humanity grieves the Spirit, but the new humanity is transformed by the Spirit. This transformation takes time, but it is essential.

I remember forty years ago when I joined the Marine Corps as a teenage boy right out of high school. A week after I graduated, I was in boot camp in San Diego. They cut off my hair. They then gave me uniforms. And a paper bag. They told me to take all my civilian clothes and put them in the paper bag and put on the uniform of a Marine. The transformation was not immediate. It took a few months to become a Marine. But the transformation was so total, so complete, when I got off a plane to come home for leave after boot camp, my mom walked right by me and didn't recognize me.

When we put off the old and put on the new, it's not immediate. It is a process, but the first step to a transformed life is a renewed mind. And the way to have a renewed mind—not darkened and walking in the futile paths of the blind—is to know Jesus Christ. And I trust that you do know Him, but if you don't, I encourage you to reach out and simply ask the Lord to forgive you of your sins and by faith receive the grace He has given to us through His Son, Jesus Christ, in His death on the cross.

Questions for Reflection and Discussion

1. Who did the Lord give to equip the saints for the work of ministry (see vv. 11–12)?

2. How are we to respond to one another (see v. 29)?
    a. Be kind.
    b. Be tenderhearted.
    c. Be forgiving.
    d. All the above.

Notes on Today's Bible Reading

— DAY 6 —

Today's Reading: Ephesians 5

Verse of the Day

> For you were once darkness, but now you are light in the
> Lord. Walk as children of light.
>
> *Ephesians 5:8*

Please read the entire Scripture selection in your own Bible and highlight
or underline verses that stand out to you before you read the observations
and engage the questions below.

In today's study, we are looking at chapter 5. Again, in this second half of the book of Ephesians, Paul covered the function of the church. Our key verse is Ephesians 5:8, which says, "For you were once darkness, but now you are light in the Lord. Walk as children of light." Having laid out the doctrine, the foundation of the church, in the first three chapters of Ephesians, Paul systematically instructed believers on the function of the church, meaning how they should live as followers of Jesus in a society that was in every way corrupted—morally, spiritually, politically, and culturally.

We read in chapter 4 that, for us as well, there must be a break with the past, a change of mind, a change of clothing per se: "put off the old humanity, put on the new humanity." And in chapter 5, we are talking about what that new humanity looks like. How does a new person in Christ conduct himself or herself? That's what we're looking at in verses 1–13.

This chapter begins with the word *Therefore*, which means it is a continuation of Paul's previous discussion of breaking with the past and no longer walking in the futility of the mind as the world does. But how do we do that? Paul told the Ephesians at the very beginning of verse 1: "Be imitators of God," or better yet, Jesus. I think the message Paul conveyed in terms of the function of the church is we are *of* the light, we are *for* the light, and we should *be* light. So, we come from God where we're the product of Jesus Christ. We should therefore live for God, for the light. And as a result, we should be light in the world.

Look at verse 8 again: "For you were once darkness, but now you are light in the Lord. Walk as children of light." See, we are the light; we are of the light. In John 8:12 Jesus said, "I am the light of the world. He who follows Me shall not walk in darkness, but have the light of life." So we are of the light, but we are also to be living for the light.

In Matthew 5:14 Jesus said, "You are the light of the world. A city that is set on a hill cannot be hidden." You see, we expose the darkness not necessarily with our words but through our lives, by the way we conduct ourselves. Look what Paul said in Ephesians 5:7–11: "Therefore do not be partakers with them. For you were once darkness, but now you are light in the Lord. Walk as children of light (for the fruit of the Spirit is in all goodness, righteousness, and truth), finding out what is acceptable to the Lord. And have no fellowship with the unfruitful works of darkness, but rather expose them." And we expose them by the way we live according to the truth, regardless of what the culture says.

Where old things have passed away, we put off the old self, and we put on the new spiritual self. And how do we do this? We become imitators of Christ. We are of the light when we are born again, when we accept Jesus Christ as our Lord and Savior. He says, "Look, I'm the Light of the world, and when you accept me, you are a part of the light. We have been bought with a price. So we're to live for the light, we're to walk as children of the light, and as a result, we become light to the world around us.

Then look at verses 14–16: "Therefore He says: 'Awake, you who sleep, arise from the dead, and Christ will give you light.' See then that you walk circumspectly, not as fools but as wise, redeeming the time, because the days are evil." Now, I find Paul's encouragement fascinating: "redeeming the time." It's almost like a transaction, an investment. Getting a return. Making the most of the time.

We often read the verse about how the days are evil, and we think of all the things happening now. Yes, these are certainly evil times; I don't dispute that. But that's not really what it's saying. Life is filled with challenges, with obstacles, in this fallen world, and those are going to come. But there are going to be times when we have an opportunity to make the most of the moment, to redeem the time. Maybe it's to share the gospel with someone. Maybe it's to take on a missionary project. It really can be anything the Lord is leading us to do. The next verse tells us how to do that. Look at Ephesians 5:17: "Therefore do not be unwise, but understand what the will of the Lord is." And how do we do this? How do we know what the will of God is? Well, we must be in the Word of God.

Look at verse 18: "And do not be drunk with wine, in which is dissipation; but be filled with the Spirit." So why is this mention of alcohol suddenly in the middle of this? That's not really what he's talking about. He's telling us not to waste our time. "Be wise, be filled with the Spirit." How do people become drunk? Well, they drink alcohol, and they are active participants. How are we filled with the Holy Spirit? We must be filling ourselves with the things of the Spirit. Paul said we're sealed by the Holy Spirit. When we're saved, we receive the Holy Spirit; we're sealed in the day of redemption. That's what I believe the Scripture says. But the degree to which we're filled with the Holy Spirit—influenced by, led by— is determined by how we yield ourselves to and fill our lives with the Holy Spirit through the reading of the Word, through prayer, through the speaking to one another in psalms and hymns and spiritual songs, singing, and making a melody in our heart to the Lord.

Then verse 20 says, "Giving thanks always for all things to God the Father in the name of our Lord Jesus Christ." Thanksgiving is really at the heart of this new life. Remember, Paul wrote from prison, "In everything give thanks; for this is the will of God in Christ Jesus for you" (1 Thess. 5:18). A key part of this is putting off the old self, putting on the new self, and having a heart of gratitude. It is powerful when we walk in gratitude and thanksgiving to the Lord, and this helps us redeem the time. Because if we're not thankful, we become angry, we're bitter because of the evil days, because of the difficult things we face. But when we are praying and we're thankful, even for the evil days, we are then understanding the will of God.

In verse 21, Paul introduced this idea of "submitting to one another in the fear of God." Here he's talking about an attitude of giving and cooperating, assuming responsibility, and carrying a burden. Then Paul brought up a subject that has created controversy when he said in verse 22, "Wives, submit to your own husbands as to the Lord." The word *submit* can be used in a military connotation, which is an order like "get in line" or "close ranks," or it can be used in a more informal way like "follow me." Paul was asking wives to submit in this way. So first, instead of having to submit to everyone, wives were under the covering of their husbands: "submit to your own husbands, as to the Lord. For the husband is the head of the wife, as also Christ is head of the church; and He is the Savior of the body."

Then there is the word to the husbands in verse 25: "Husbands, love your wives, just as Christ also loved the church and gave Himself for her." Look at this in the context of the way Jesus operates. If a husband is to operate as Jesus did, Jesus said to those whom He invited to become His disciples, "Deny yourself, take up your cross and follow me." I can tell you right now the nature of God is not to demand that anyone follows Him. Jesus doesn't demand that we follow Him. He invites us to follow Him, and then we submit to His leadership because we're following Him. That's what it's describing here. It's not ordering military structure, which I'll have to be honest, I didn't really get when I was first married.

My wife and I had some challenges in our early years, and a lot of it was because I was still in the Marine Corps. I thought I could run my family—which was just my wife and me at the time—as I did a platoon. And I was wrong. That's not the way it worked. Once I came to understand this passage in chapter 5, it really changed how I looked at marriage and our relationship. I saw I was to love my wife as Christ loved the church, literally, selflessly giving everything up, leaving heaven and all the riches and glory of heaven to come to this earth and live, so He might redeem us and make us into what He wants us to be—a bride. And it was through this I understood that, yes, I had a problem in our marriage. But it wasn't my wife; it was me.

As husbands begin to lead sacrificially and wives submit to that loving leadership, it works beautifully. This is why it's crucial that husbands and wives have a relationship with Jesus Christ because that's the center. Without this transformative relationship of following Christ, it doesn't work. I know you can make it work, but it's difficult. My wife and I have been married for thirty-six years, and it's wonderful. It gets better every day because both of us are submitted to Christ and following in that way.

When we accept Jesus Christ as our Lord and Savior, we are filled with the Spirit, and under His controlling influence, we're able to submit to one another in the body. We can function lovingly in marriage and seize opportunities where we recognize we are of the light, we live for the light, and as a result, we are light to the world around us. So today, let's live as light!

Questions for Reflection and Discussion

1. Based on the analogy Paul gave, what does it mean to be "filled with the Spirit" (see v. 18)?

2. How is the marital relationship like the relationship between Christ and His church (vv. 25–32)?
   a. Wives are to submit to their husbands like the church to the Lord.
   b. Husbands are to love their wives like Christ loved the church and gave Himself sacrificially for her.
   c. Both of the above
   d. Neither of the above

Notes on Today's Bible Reading

— DAY 7 —

Today's Reading: Ephesians 6

Verse of the Day

> Therefore take up the whole armor of God, that you may
> be able to withstand in the evil day, and having done all, to
> stand.
>
> *Ephesians 6:13*

Please read the entire Scripture selection in your own Bible and highlight
or underline verses that stand out to you before you read the observations
and engage the questions below.

Ephesians 6 is one of my favorite chapters in all the Scriptures.
If you tune into "Washington Watch," you will recall that I
sign off every day with Ephesians 6:13, my life verse and our key
verse for today's study: "Therefore take up the whole armor of God,
that you may be able to withstand in the evil day, and having done
all, to stand."

In our previous study, we saw how Paul spoke of the trans-
forming power of God's Spirit (5:18), whose controlling influence
should permeate every area of life. This includes our devotional
relationship with God in worship and thanksgiving (5:19–20), our
respectful relationships with fellow church members (5:21), and
our marital relationship (5:22–33).

The emphasis on the Spirit's influence continues in chapter 6 with our family relationships between parents and children and a special word to fathers (6:1–4). Paul included in this section a word about workplace relationships between servant and master, or as we think today, between employee and employer (6:5–9). Finally, Paul concluded the letter with the call to stand firm in the spiritual battle raging all around us, armed with God's strength, clothed with His armor, and persevering in prayer (6:10–20).

Let's dive in and look at 6:1–4. Speaking of the parent-child relationship, notice Paul instructed children first to obey then honor (vv. 1–3). There may be occasions when obedience is not possible, but honor is unconditional, and God will bless that honor. Pay close attention to this next verse, which is also a command: "Fathers do not provoke your children to wrath" (v. 4a). That's the negative side of a father's potential influence.

I saw this headline recently: "Our greatest public health crisis? The angry young American male."[3] Others have pointed to the increase in mass shootings perpetrated by angry young men. Why might they be angry? The anger can often be traced to a rejection from their fathers, who either were never in their lives, walked out, or were emotionally absent. The notion promoted that fathers are not essential to children is another one of those lies from the pit of hell. A father's presence and positive influence are absolutely critical to the success of children.

In fact, this brings us to the positive part of Paul's command to fathers regarding their children: "but bring them up in the training and admonition of the Lord" (v. 4b). It is imperative that fathers fulfill their biblical role to instruct, to encourage, and most importantly, to be an example to their children. This is one of the reasons the Family Research Council launched our Stand Courageous men's conferences a few years ago. We realized if men would follow the Lord, serve Him, and lead their families to do the same, we could solve most of the social pathologies in our nation. Spiritually engaged fathers leading their families are the key.

The next relationship Paul spoke about in 6:5–9 is between servants and masters, which we apply today to the workplace. We are to do our work "as unto the Lord." And I have found this to be quite freeing in the various environments I've been in throughout my career. I've worked for some tough people, and I've worked for some people who didn't appreciate what I did and didn't recognize it. But I realized that I work for the Lord, and He is my boss. Consequently, we should work just as it says here in Ephesians 6:6–7: "not with eyeservice, as men-pleasers, but as bondservants of Christ, doing the will of God from the heart, with goodwill doing service, as to the Lord, and not to men." Knowing this is the key. Whatever good anyone does, he will receive the same from the Lord, whether he is slave or free. When we begin to realize we work for God and He's the one who will bring the increase, bless us, and prosper us even though someone else may sign our check, that's freeing.

* * *

We conclude the book by reviewing the things Paul said we need to do: How we need to live as children of the light. How we need to walk circumspectly, not as fools but as wise children of the light, putting off the old self and putting on the new. And how the Holy Spirit should be the controlling influence in all our various relationships with God, in the church, at home, and in the workplace. Paul gave us instruction after instruction on God's design for Christian living, how we are to function as believers, which was totally counterculture then as it is now.

Now this can all seem overwhelming. How can we possibly live this way? Ready? Here it is: "Finally, my brethren, be strong in the Lord and in the power of His might" (v. 10). To live this way, we must be empowered. Our strength is found in the power of God's might. We must have His strength, His courage and boldness, or what Paul told us next will be of little use.

Consider verse 11: "Put on the whole armor of God, that you may be able to stand against the wiles of the devil." If we don't have a heart of courage, we don't have any need for battle gear. Then Paul lifted the curtain on the real enemy in verse 12: "For we do not wrestle against flesh and blood, but against principalities, against powers, against the rulers of the darkness of this age, against spiritual [hosts] of wickedness in the heavenly [places]." This one verse tells us all we need to know about what we are up against. We are *not* battling people—we are fighting against all of *hell*, against Satan and his demons. These terms Paul used are not redundant; these are levels or ranks of what we are battling against as we are in the kingdom of God going against the forces of darkness. There are demonic forces over nations and regions, cities and territories, and even some unsaved people.

How are we to deal with them? Paul told us in verse 13: "Therefore take up the whole armor of God, that you may be able to withstand in the evil day, and having done all, to stand." We are to put on the armor God has provided and boldly stand in the power of God's might through the Holy Spirit, refusing to surrender or relent. Then Paul lists the armor in verses 14–17: belt of truth, breastplate of righteousness, footgear of gospel peace, shield of faith, helmet of salvation, and the sword of the Spirit—the Word of God. Unlike the other pieces of equipment designed to protect and defend, the sword, the Word of God, is designed to take ground and go on the offensive. And notice there's no armor for our backside, meaning no retreat.

Paul went on to describe the often forgotten but one of the most powerful weapons in our arsenal: "praying always with all prayer and supplication in the Spirit, being watchful to this end with all perseverance and supplication for all the saints" (v. 18). Look at the characteristics of this prayer: (1) praying always (Paul said, "Pray without ceasing," 1 Thess. 5:17) and (2) persevering in prayer (Jesus told the parable of the widow and the politician to make the point that "men always ought to pray and not lose heart," Luke 18:1). What are we to pray for? Everything! But especially strength for ourselves and others. Look at what Paul asks for in verses 19–20: "that utterance may be given to me, that I may open my mouth boldly to make known the mystery of the gospel, for which I am an ambassador in chains; that in it I may speak boldly, as I ought to speak."

This is incredible. Paul was already bold, but he is asking for more boldness. Why was Paul in prison? For speaking boldly! Now he is asking for prayer so that he will continue to speak boldly. When I think of Paul, I don't think of timid, weak, or afraid. Yet I think Paul is being transparent in his request for boldness. There are times when we all get weary in the battle, and frankly, we want to step back, sit down, and go silent. We can't—too much is at stake! We need to pray for our leaders that they remain bold and courageous, inspiring others to do the same.

What a great chapter. Be strong in the Lord. The Christian life must be lived in the strength and the power of the Lord Jesus Christ. Be aware of what we are fighting against. It is not against flesh and blood. It is not a battle between Left and Right. It's not a battle between Republican and Democrat. It's not that complicated or confusing. In fact, it's really simple. It's a battle between good and evil. It's light against darkness. How do we fight this spiritual battle? With spiritual weapons. Be prayed up, be equipped with the spiritual gear from God, be bold and committed to stand the ground God has entrusted to us.

Going back to my days in the Marine Corps and even in law enforcement, we had to have the right equipment. Our equipment not only protected us, but it gave us the ability to perform the mission and the task we had been assigned. But all the weapons in the world are no substitute for courage and the strength that only comes from the Lord. Jesus said the devil's mission is to lie and steal, kill and destroy. Our mission is to follow the Lord Jesus Christ, take the fight to Satan, and take the light of Christ into the darkness that others might come to know Him and be set free from spiritual bondage. That challenge grows greater with each passing day. The way to turn the tide is to take our stand. Then having prayed, prepared, and taken our stand, by all means, keep on standing!

Questions for Reflection and Discussion

1. What special parenting instructions are specifically given to fathers (see v. 4)?

2. What does the armor of God allow us to do (see vv. 11–14)?
   a. Take our stand against the devil's schemes
   b. When the day of evil comes, we may be able to stand our ground, and after having done everything, to stand.
   c. Stand firm
   d. All the above

Notes on Today's Bible Reading

Appendix 1:
Stand on the Word Bible Reading Plan

Visit frc.org/Bible for our chronological journey through the Bible that we call "Stand on the Word." We encourage you to spend time reading and studying the Bible because it is literally "God-breathed" (2 Tim. 3:16); it is God's very words to us. The Bible answers the big questions, such as, Why am I here? Where did I come from? Where am I going (life after death)? If God is good, why does evil and suffering exist? The Bible not only answers these big questions; it offers practical advice in areas such as, How can I deal with feelings of fear or anger or guilt? How can I forgive when I cannot forget? What should I look for in a spouse? How can I have a successful marriage? How can I be a good parent? What is my spiritual gift and place in the church? What is my stewardship responsibility as a citizen? We learned the verse in Bible school, "Your word is a lamp to my feet and a light to my path" (Ps. 119:105). God's Word shows us the way forward in any area of life and on every question we face.

The Stand on the Word Bible Reading Plan takes us through the Bible chronologically. In other words, each reading takes you through the Bible as events occurred in history as far as it is possible. Here is how it works for our family. At the same time each morning, whether I am at home, in Washington, or some foreign country, I send my wife and children a morning greeting along with a reminder of the passage for the day. The text includes two questions related to the reading. The questions are designed to help in content retention, serve as an accountability tool, and provide for discussion.

The two-year plan does not have a Sunday passage. Instead, it provides an outline for a family discussion that can be done on Sunday afternoon or evening each week. The weekly discussion time begins with a spiritual leader asking each person individually for one or two insights or truths they gained from their reading during the week. After everyone else shares, you can then lead a short discussion based upon one of the passages that you read in the week just completed. It is also a time for them to ask questions.

By the way, you don't have to have all the answers. If you don't know, tell them so, then talk to your pastor or other trusted person with Bible knowledge. If your children start asking questions, that suggests they are thinking about what they are reading.

Reading God's Word will help you establish a fruitful walk with the God who made you and loves you. Whether you are single or married, this plan will enable you to lead your friends and family in daily reading God's Word. The added benefit is that you will all be reading the same text together. It will amaze you to see how God speaks sometimes in the same ways and at other times in different ways to each of you. Being on this journey together will build a spiritual synergy, a deep bond, and sense of unity and purpose like nothing else! Use it to impart the Word of life.

Appendix 2:
Prayer: Talking with God

Most Americans say they pray. But not as many pray the way Jesus did, the way He taught His disciples to pray. Fewer still really know the power in prayer God gave us to impact our families, communities, nation, and world. Prayer is our lifeline to God, our means of communicating with our heavenly Father. It develops our relationship—our friendship, fellowship, and intimacy with Him. In prayer we experience God and are "filled with the Spirit" (see Eph. 5:18–21). God uses the prayers of faithful men, women, boys, and girls to heal broken lives and strengthen families, churches, communities, and even nations. He uses our prayers to advance his Kingdom on earth (Daniel 9; Acts 4:36). He wants to use all believers!

The Essence of Prayer

Prayer is simply talking with God—about anything and everything. He is our Maker, Father, Savior, Provider, and Counselor; our Master, Healer, Guide, and Friend. Christ died for our sins and rose from the dead to sit at the right hand of God the Father, where He is praying for us right now (Heb. 10:12). His Spirit now lives within us and helps us to pray (1 John 4:16).

The Priority of Prayer

Jesus spent time alone with God regularly drawing strength from the Father and seeking His will for every decision (Luke 6:12–13; 22:39–44). His disciples asked Jesus to teach them how to pray (Luke 11:1–13). The apostles knew that prayer and obedience were the keys to Christ's life and ministry and were determined to follow His example: "[W]e will devote ourselves to prayer and to the ministry of the word" (Acts 6:4). Too few American men pray today, even pastors and leaders! Yet strong praying men are the norm in Scripture. Our families, churches, and nation need men who will make prayer a priority today! (1 Tim. 2:8).

The Practice of Prayer

Scripture teaches, "Pray continually!" (1 Thess. 5:17); "Pray always" (Eph. 6:18); "Always pray and do not give up" (Luke 18:1). Below are some helps to get you started. No one can beat the Lord's Prayer. It is an outline of key themes to guide our prayer lives: "Our Father in heaven, hallowed be your name. Your kingdom come, your will be done, on earth as it is in heaven. Give us this day our daily bread, and forgive us our debts, as we also have forgiven our debtors. And lead us not into temptation, but deliver us from evil" (Matt. 6:9–13).

In the book of Psalms and throughout Scripture, God has sprinkled prayers/patterns for us to learn from. Here is a simple, popular acronym to help jog our memories.

P-R-A-Y:

- *Praise:* Our Father which art in heaven, hallowed be thy name.
- *Repent:* And forgive us our debts, as we forgive our debtors.
- *Ask:* Give us this day our daily bread. And forgive us our debts, as we forgive our debtors. And lead us not into temptation but deliver us from evil.
- *Yield:* Thy kingdom come. Thy will be done in earth, as it is in heaven.

Praying through Scripture

God also talks to us. The Bible is His Word (2 Tim. 2:15; 3:16). Bible in hand, we should pray God's promises back to Him and claim them for our families, our work, our finances, and our nation (1 Tim. 2:1–8; 1 John 5:14–15).

Scriptures to Pray as a Man: Joshua 1:8; 1 Timothy 3:1–15; 1 Chronicles 12:32; 1 Timothy 6:1–12; 1 Corinthians 16:13; Romans 12:1–21; Micah 6:8; John 4:24; Acts 2:38: 1 Kings 2:2; Ephesians 5:25–28; Genesis 2:24; 1 Peter 3:7; Ephesians 4:26–27; Matthew 5:32; Proverbs 5:19; 1 Corinthians 6:18; Deuteronomy 4:8–10; 11:18–21; Exodus 34:5–8; Psalm 127:3–5; Matthew 7:11; Ephesians 6:4; Proverbs 22:6; Luke 11:11–12; Hebrews 12:5–7

Scriptures to Pray as a Woman: Matthew 22:36–40; Proverbs 31:30; 1 Peter 3:1–3; Ephesians 5:26; Ephesians 4:15, 29; 1 Timothy 3:11; Ephesians 5:22, 24; 1 Peter 3:1–2; Philippians 4:10–13; Philippians 2:3–4; Proverbs 31:12; 1 Corinthians 7:34; Titus 2:3–4; Titus 2:4–5; James 1:19; Ephesians 4:32; 1 Corinthians 7:1–5; Luke 2:37; Colossians 4:2; Proverbs 31:27; 1 Timothy 5:14; 1 Timothy 5:14

Scriptures to Pray for Your Children: Matthew 22:36–40; 2 Timothy 3:15; Psalm 97:10, 38:18; Proverbs 8:13; John 17:15, 10:10; Romans 12:9; Psalm 119:71; Hebrews 12:5–6; Daniel 1:17, 20; Proverbs 1:4; James 1:5; Romans 13:1; Ephesians 6:1–3; Hebrews 13:17; Proverbs 1:10–16; 13:20; 2 Corinthians 6:14–17; Deuteronomy 6; 1 Corinthians 6:18–20; Acts 24:16; 1 Timothy 1:19,4:1–2; Titus 1:15–16; Psalm 23:4; Deuteronomy 10:12; Matthew 28:18–20; Ephesians 1:3, 4:29; Ephesians 1:16–19; Philippians 1:11; Colossians 1:9; Philippians 1:9–10

Developing Personal Prayer Habits

Rise early each day to pray with opened Bible. Daniel prayed three times daily. Pray whenever you can: as you drive, with your wife, with your children at dinner and before bedtime. You cannot pray too much!

Praying Together with Others

Pray with your spouse regularly. Make time for family prayer. Be part of your church prayer meeting or group. Christ said, "My house shall be called a house of prayer" (Matt. 21:13). The apostle Paul instructed Pastor Timothy to make prayer the first order of the church, saying prayer is key to peace in the nation (1 Tim. 2:1–8). There is nothing like a Spirit-led prayer meeting with people who love the Lord! Praying women have been standing in the prayer gap for decades. Every man must set his heart to become a praying man, lead his family in prayer, and be a strong contributor to the corporate prayer life of his church. We must be leaders in praying for our morally and spiritually troubled, divided nation—and for our national leaders. American Christians simply must respond to God's promise: "If My people who are called by My name will humble themselves, and pray and seek My face, and turn from their wicked ways, then I will hear from heaven, and will forgive their sin and heal their land" (2 Chron. 7:14).

Prayer As Warfare

Jesus described the enemy, the devil, as a thief whose mission is to "steal, kill and destroy" (John 10:10). Demonic forces are at war against everything good in you, your family, your church, your community, America, and every nation (Ephesians 6:10–20).

The devil and his minions are out to thwart the kingdom of God and eliminate righteousness wherever he can. He hates God and hates people and will use spiritually ignorant and deceived men, women, boys, and girls to do his bidding. Men of God today, like the sons of Issachar in ancient Israel, need to understand the times and know what the church and our nation must do (1 Chron. 12:32). We must pull down Satan's strongholds, wrestle for our families, and use Spirit-led prayer and wisdom to help guide our churches and communities to prevail against the evil onslaught against us (2 Cor. 10:3–5). This is the war of the ages, and it is real.

Finally, Determine to Become a Person of Prayer

No matter how long you have been a Christian and may have neglected prayer up until now, you can become a person of prayer starting today. If you have missed the mark, it is not too late. Call upon the Lord, ask for His help, and proceed with His guidance. O Lord, make me a praying person; make me a prayer warrior! In Jesus's name, amen!

Notes

1. "Daily Devotional: Can anything separate you from God?," Love Worth Finding, April 5, 2019, https://www.lwf.org/daily-devotions/can-anything-separate-you-from-god.

2. "Eight Words That Can Transform Your Life," Dale Carnegie Way, March 11, 2013, https://dalecarnegiewaynj.com/2013/03/11/eight-words-that-can-transform-your-life/.

3. Maureen Callahan, "Our greatest public health crisis? The angry young American male," *New York Post*, May 25, 2022, https://nypost.com/2022/05/25/our-greatest-public-health-crisis-the-angry-young-american-male/.

Also available from
Fidelis Publishing and Family Research Council

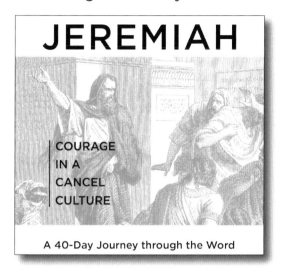

STAND on the WORD Study Guides

Jeremiah: Courage
in a Cancel Culture
ISBN: 9781956454369

Nehemiah:
Rebuilding a Nation
ISBN: 9781956454468

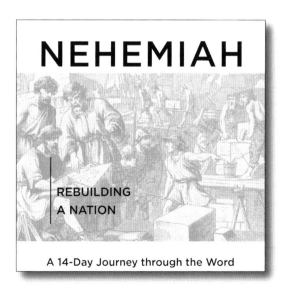